MY PAPA
Copyright © 2022 Warren Edward Morris
All rights reserved.

No part of this book may be reproduced, stored in retrieval systems, or transmitted in any form, by any means, including mechanical, electronic, photocopying, recording or otherwise, without prior written permission of the author.

ISBN 13: 978-1-7366170-5-2
LCCN: 2021903542

Illustrations and Design by Taillefer Long
info@IlluminatedStories.com

I dedicated this book to my mother Jessie, who showed me unconditional love as both my mother and father while ensuring I had the spiritual, mental, and physical guidance necessary to grow into the person I am today.

May you rest in peace, Mom. Love You Always!

To the Morris Family for your support and love.

Hello my name is Morgan,

I am 8 years old and in the third grade.

I live in Virginia with my mother, father, and two brothers, Xzavier and Alexander, plus my dog Odie.

I am a dancer!

I would like to share a great story about me and my grandfather. I call him Papa.

He is the best person ever.

My story begins when Papa took me and Xzavier on our first plane ride to visit family in Alabama.

I was excited, happy, and scared.

My Papa sat next to me on the plane and held my hand.

I was not afraid anymore.

We flew to Gadsden, Alabama,
where My Papa grew up,
to attend a family reunion.

He introduced us to great aunts, uncles, and cousins.

Another trip My Papa took Xzavier and I on was to the Smithsonian National Museum of African American History and Culture in Washington, D.C.

We dance together.
He attends my dance recitals.

He takes Xzavier and I to the movies.

He attends church with us.

He takes us to fancy places to eat.

He reads with me.
He listens to me.
He mentors me.

He treats me SPECIAL.

I enjoy the time I spend with Papa maybe when my little brother Alexander is older, he can join Xzavier and I on trips with Papa.

He shows me so much love.

I am so blessed to have My Papa.

ABOUT THE AUTHOR

Warren Edward Morris is a program manager with the United States Navy, whose passion is mentoring and empowering individuals. With his business management education from Upper Iowa University as well as his professional credentials and unique life experiences, he serves as a great example of how hard work and dedication open doors to endless possibilities.

He currently lives in Northern Virginia and is the president and founder of With Essential Means, LLC, a consulting company dedicated to teaching young people how to become role models in the way they act, speak, and dress, instilling confidence in them while inspiring them to realize their power. When not writing, Warren enjoys traveling and sharing experiences with his grandchildren, Morgan, Xzavier, and Alexander.

Visit Warren's website to learn more about With Essential Means, LLC at withessentialmeans.com.

www.ingramcontent.com/pod-product-compliance
Lightning Source LLC
Chambersburg PA
CBHW042255100526
44589CB00002B/30